Sparkling Deep Waters

Poems & Prose
Inspired by God

Karen J Chisholm

Inks and Bindings
888-290-5218
www.inksandbindings.com
orders@inksandbindings.com

This Book is Dedicated

To the Glory of God

It could change your life!

Books by Karen J Chisholm

I AM with You
Poems Inspired by God

Tough as Nails
Poems Inspired by God

Voices
Poems Inspired by God

In Green Pastures
Poems Inspired by God

Red Redeems
Poems Inspired by God

Contents

Section 1

Deep Moments with God

Section 2
Jesus

Section 3
Father

Section 4
Believing

DEEP MOMENTS WITH GOD

Sparkling Deep Waters
Deep Moments with God

Sparkling, catching, reflecting the light
Words that point in joy to God
Are sparkling.
Godly wisdom shared and poured
Brings joy to hearers never bored
Who know and love and hear the Lord
And worship . . . Giving praise . . . To God.

I delight in these beloved,
Ones who seek to know Me, find me,
I will lead them to My Presence.
There they will find rest.
I refresh them and they go
To the world, its ebb and flow,
Carry My Word as they grow
In Grace . . . In wisdom . . . Blessed.

When you meet them, you'll meet Me
For they carry Me inside.
You will know them by their fruit . . .
Love, joy, peace, patience,
Kindness, goodness, faithfulness,
Gentleness, self-control.
They wait . . . on Me . . . My servants.

"The words of a discreet and wise man's mouth are like deep waters,
plenteous and difficult to fathom, and the fountain of skillful and godly
wisdom is like a gushing.
Proverbs 18:4 Amp

A Moment to Focus

Lord, I focus on You.
I draw nigh and let all thought go.
I seek your presence,
I seek your face,
And just for a bit,
My soul reaches out to You.

And I am rewarded with your peace
Gently filling me, flowing through me,
Filling all the worry places,
Helping me let go of the now
And connect with the forever
Where you alone are King.

With all my thoughts suspended,
And all my doubts upended,
I know I am with Jesus.
And just for a moment . . .
We are one.

Then I turn and face my day
With calm assurance You are with me,
And Your joy is my strength.
As I go forward into what the day brings
I have no fear as I walk in Your light
Because I took a moment to focus.

Begin to Fathom

Aren't you a child of God?
Aren't you saved by the blood of the Lamb?
Then you have the right to come
To the throne of grace where you
Are welcomed with open arms.
Or you may say "I'm not comfortable
Praying out loud in public."
Well, I'm not either.

There have been times that I was praying what
seemed to be impossible things, and my heart
Was backing down because I was asking
For things I couldn't make happen,
Things that had never happened in my lifetime.
And Holy Spirit showed me that
If I were only asking for what I could do
Or what had happened before, I was putting
God in a box.

He told me I had made Him over in my image so I could in some way understand Him and know what to expect. Then He let me know He refuses to have limits set on Him and He refuses to meet my expectations, and if I was going to pray to Him, I was the one who was going to have to change. He told me to begin to fathom.

He wants us to ask bigger.
I looked up the word 'fathom'.
It is a measure to test the depth
of the ocean.

It is also the measure of
The span of a man's arms.
In the old languages,
Fath meant father.
Om meant arm.
He wants us to pray using the
measure of God the Father's
Arms.

That means nothing is impossible!
We can ask for *anything* in Jesus'
Name and He will do it
When it aligns with His will.

Anything!

So now I come running
to God for anything.
When I see a need,
I ask God to meet it.

When I hear of sickness
or trouble, I look to God
and ask BIG!

I ignore my feelings of
inadequacy because
I don't have to make the
prayers come true.
God will do it according to
His purpose.

My job is to open my mouth
and ask,
Making my requests known
to God.
You may say
"Don't you think God already
knows what we want?"

Yes, He does.

But His Word tells us to ask
And keep on asking,
To knock and keep on knocking.

He says at some point,
The door will be opened to us.
So, begin to fathom and see what
God wants to do through you.

Are you a child of God?
If not, today is your day to accept
and
Believe Jesus died for sinners
To have a way out,
A way to come to God.

Just ask.

Then . . .

Begin to fathom.

Unchanging

Rock of ages, Everlasting Rock.
I shall not be moved Rock.
Lord God.

You are constant, unchanging.
No shadow of turning.
The same yesterday, today,
And forever.

You do not change
But You repented of
Anger that annihilates,
Are willing to reason
Together with man.

Who is man
That You are mindful of him?
Your creation,
Made in Your image.

You breathed Your life
Into the nostrils of the first man.
You made him from
The dust of the earth:
Carbon.

You made the first man
To please You.
Carbon copy.

You put Your spirit in him,
Making him a living soul.

You gave him dominion
Over the earth,
Over the animals,
Over this world You created.

You made of his rib
A helpmeet, a mate,
A woman, created
Out of Your Carbon copy.

And when they ate
Of the fruit denied them,
You came looking for them

You covered them,
Covered their disobedience
With the skins of
Animals You sacrificed.

They didn't know
Sacrifice atones.

But You taught them
What pleased you:
The offering,
The rules of offerings.

They knew
That the offering of life
Is the only acceptable
Gift of worship.

They taught their children.
Abel knew.
Cain knew.
And later Seth would learn.

They knew that living blood
Was the offering
You would accept.

You gave the Law
On Sinai to Moses.
All the rules,
Recorded too.

The laws on rock
The rules of keeping
Worship holy
You gave to man.

They became
Your chosen people.
Out of Israel,
Twelve tribes
And Levites
Blessed by Your hand.

And then the time,
The years completed,
You sent Your Son,
Fulfilled the Law.

Long prophesied,
Yearned and awaited,
Unrecognized in the
Baby they saw.

Both God and man,
The Bridge between worlds.
Spirit and flesh
Met there in Him.

Perfection offered
Obeyed and taught,
Was crucified:
God in the skin of man.

And living blood
At last was offered
That satisfied
All Laws' demands.

Fulfilled the Promise,
And brought Your kingdom
To the strait path opened
Between heaven and man.

The Prince of Peace
Triumphed and won.
And the Prince of this world,
Became defeated foe.

Foe of the Father,
Hater of mankind,
Deceiver sentenced,
To fire would go.

Until the Judgment,
He's still deceiving
So men won't want
God's sacrifice.

Tricked ones wander
Until they die here.
Deceiver uses
Any device.

If he can't be God,
Then nor will men
Gain place in heaven
Where he once dwelt.

Cast out for treason
Has a vendetta
'Gainst God's little images,
Resents man will know
Glory he felt.

Father will do
All He has promised.
Through His Son,
Be glorified.

And every man who
Believes and serves Him
Will see His Glory,
Watch by His side

Because these little
Carbon copies
Believe the Truth
Is Jesus.

Love Does Not

It does not. No. It doesn't.
Love does not run away; it hangs in there.
Love is looking for the good that will follow.
Love believes in happy endings, so it waits,
Believing in good.

Love does not envy. It is generous
And appreciates another's blessings,
Rejoicing for that one's joy.
Love does not play games.

Jealousy doesn't live here, for there is no
Room within love to be jealous.
Love would have to cease, to stop,
To allow jealousy any room at all.
No, Love doesn't thrive
Where there is jealousy.

Love does not boast. It doesn't.
It has no need to draw attention to itself,
For it is complete, having more than enough
So it can generously give love away.

Love cannot be puffed up,
For it does not even need to be noticed.
Love is self-provisioning. It is enough.
It does not need. It gives.

Love does not behave rudely
Because it never insists on it rights.
It *is* right.

Love does not seek its own.
It *is* its own, having all it needs,
Every requirement satisfied,
Always ready to focus on others.

Love does not become provoked.
Love does not entertain negative thoughts.
It remains focused on loving
In positive, healthy, live-giving ways,

And negativity withers.

Love does not think on nor dwell on evil.
There is simply no interest.
Darkness and light cannot dwell together.

Love does not get pleasure
From another's misfortune.
To do that, Love would
Have to be needy itself.
And it isn't.

Love bears all things,
Not with a "this too shall pass" attitude,
But believing all things work together
For good to them that love.

Love always hopes.
Always.
It never weakens.

Love does not fail. It is perfect.
It is, in fact, the only thing in this world
That *is* perfect.

God is Love.

> I Corinthians 13 4-7
> Romans 8:28
> John 4:8

Waiting

How do I wait upon You, Lord?
Quietly passing the time?
Making a choice, then hearing your voice
Or crafting myself worthless rhyme?

Trusting You'll meet me, I come,
Sit in my chair, hope I'll *hear*.
What have I done? Why should you come
Answer my prayer and draw near?

Child, I AM with you right here in your chair.
I'm close as breath; dwell inside.
Here, you have all of Me you'll ever need.
There is no thought you can hide.

Waiting holds promise receiving will come
When you are talking to Me.
Stopping to look up and smile says it all:
Happy to come and just be.

I will reward all those willing to wait,
While quietly opening self.
Make Myself known,
My words understood.
You will find I AM your help.

Keep waiting.

My Music in You

Child, this is the day I've made;
I've planned this day to spend with you.
I'm singing songs your spirit knows.
Today you hear me sing to you.

I give the songs for those who hear
And every day give more.
All music comes from Me to you
From all I have in store.

Some people hear and understand
I'm the Giver of the song.
Others assume it's theirs alone,
To them their art belongs.

And I'm unmoved and unsurprised.
I give yet more to those who hear,
For in the end, each one will know.
Some will bow and some shed tears.

Music in Me expressed through you,
Each one I try that hears Me too,
And some believe, step out in faith
While others wait, they hesitate,
Forget the song by waiting long,

But today . . . I sing to you.

JESUS

First Love

All I AM is before you,
Standing here among.
In My Glory, I implore you,
Complete what you've begun.

Once you came, broken, crying,
Wretched, could not stand.
'Twas your spirit bleeding, dying.
I reached out My hand.

I heard your cries, a prayer petition,
Drew you close to Me.
In the wonder of My Presence
Your finite eyes could see.

Love was reaching, had been ever,
You held out *your* hand.
I brought healing, sin to sever.
Saved, you then could stand.

Closer to Me, you came seeking,
New life you then led.
Hungry, in My Word was feasting.
Scripture was your bread.

Daily time you gave Me then
Brought closeness: Me in you.
My Presence with you seen by men,
My Glory, others drew.

Here today I live within you,
Your life is push and shove
Soft, My Spirit oft reminds too
I AM your First Love.

Meet Me early in the quiet.
Linger in My Presence.
Know I'm with you, don't deny it,
Here renew life's essence.

Wisdom, strength, and power of faith
Grow stronger 'neath My touch.
When you start your day with Me,
Your life is full of such.

Keep self free and unentangled,
Heart attuned above.
Let the worries all be wrangled
By your heart's First Love.

As you praise Me and you worship,
Peace completely fills.
Spirit with you softens slip,
Calm assurance stills.

Early mornings with your First Love
Puts Me in your day.
I AM then the heart and soul of
You. . . I light your way.

Come early
    To linger
        With Me.

Jesus

Assurance

Beloved, I AM with you.
Whether you have a clear mind to the
end or sit silent and vacant when I come
for you, I AM with you.

No matter what is before you,
I will be with you throughout,
And I will still be holding your hand
As you walk into heaven.

Trust me. Believe Me when I say
I will never leave you or forsake you.
Remember, I will not leave you
Comfortless. I will come to you.

I do not change. I AM Truth. I AM Light.
With Me is no shadow of turning.
It is forever now in My Presence,
And I AM with you always,
Even to the end of the age.

Life begins for each one after a long wait
And an unwelcome trauma.
Life ends for many with trauma
And a long wait.

For others, it is an instant change,
A surprise, a *suddenly!*

Keep your focus on Me.
Only I can bring You through the fire, Through
the flood,
Through the trials and tears and doubts
And fears, and wash you in My Blood.

You are Mine. Always Mine.
Ever, only Mine.
Nothing can separate us:
Neither life, nor death,

Nor things past, nor things to come,
Or any other thing will ever separate
You from the Love of God
Which is found fully in Me.

You can know you are saved.
You can be assured
That I have been with you
Since before conception.

I AM.   *Jesus*

Far Beyond

Much of what I do
Is beyond your understanding,
So many words
You cannot comprehend.

When your trial is heavy,
When battered and forsaken,
I AM closer than
Your heartbeat to attend.

In every part of living,
I go with you through it all.
I AM present in your joy
And suffering, hear you when you call.

I hear your worry, feel your panic,
Know your doubts and fears.
But you say Jesus! I believe!
And praise then brings Me near.

The enemy would shut you up
And close you down and stymie you.
He hates it when you
Praise Me under fire.

He wants your focus on yourself,
Wants you to fear and cower.
When you still worship Me,
He's mad; it feeds his ire.

And in the days of joy and peace,
You don't forget to love Me.
You thank Me for My Presence
Each new day.

Your trust and adulation
Bring Me glory, bring Me honor.
In or out of time,
You please Me in this way.

As you learn I'm all sufficient.
Relationship is deepened.
For every need you have,
I'm your supply.

And far beyond this moment,
You've great treasure up in
heaven: Weight of glory resting
On you in My eyes.

Jesus

Follow

Follow Me . . .
I know where we are going.

I've things to show along the way
You hadn't planned to see.
I know the path will change your life
And draw you close to Me.

There'll be places you've longed to be
And challenges requiring prayer,
And grace-filled opportunities,
And every step, I'm with you there.

Come now and follow, child of Mine.
Sometimes you wish you could just rest,
May even pine for what's behind,
And question whether I know best.

It is enough you come aside,
There's so much more for you to see.
You'll never have to leave My side,
Come close here and follow Me.

Just . . . *follow.*

Jesus

Just Love Me

Beloved, welcome into My open arms.
You build spiritual strength
When you present yourself open to Me.
You bring Me joy with your thoughts of Me.

Your spoken words to Me are often
A continuation of what you are thinking
A conversation . . .
Easily misinterpreted by others.

So what?
You are in fairly constant
Communication with Me
And that trumps everything.

Just love Me, child.
Keep on loving Me,
For I AM with you no matter what.
I PROMISE.

Jesus

Early

Here in the dark,
Shut in with Me
Your spirit is open,
Your mind and thoughts free

And that which the sunlight
Reveals to your eyes
Is hidden and holding
And can't mesmerize.

Here in the early,
Awaiting to wake,
Your mind still unfocused
Will hear, My words take.

You write in the darkness
Deep truth from My heart
And by the day breaking
You have a fresh start.

Your day goes much better
When you sacrifice
An hour of sleep to
Spend time with your Christ.

Great peace then goes with you
All the day long
Relaxed, fresh, you smile at
Whatever goes wrong.

My Presence stays with you
Wherever you go
And others may notice
You just warmly glow.

The hard knocks of life
Will not set you adrift
In worry, then grasping
To quick mend a rift.

You'll see this life's troubles
As small and will wait
As short prayer refocus
Leads you calm in faith.

It's harder to hear
My soft voice in your mind.
When morning news comes,
You leave Me behind.

So, seek in the early
While Savior awaits
To give you My Peace
To face life-storming gates.

You've nothing to lose
And all heaven to gain
As you wait in My presence
I take all your pain.

And here in the dark
I will meet you who come
In faith stepping forward
To meet with God's Son.

Fresh blessings enfold you
And grace takes your hand.
Leading and guiding
I'll cause you to stand.

Strong . . . . . .   in faith
Sure . . . .   of your salvation
True . . . .   because you want more.
Ready . . . . . .   now hidden in Christ
Knowing . . . . .   you are Mine
Remembering .   I AM with you forever.

Jesus

Pure Joy!

I love you, Beloved,
For always and ever
Past breath and past time
Ever you are Mine.

There is no other exactly like you
Though similar some souls may be
I have made you to love Me,
To serve Me, to sing
And My Spirit is all over you.

You look like Me, you talk like Me
Say all the words I speak to you.
You sound like Me, you walk like Me
You live in Me and I in you.

You have given yourself freely to Me
And offered your life for My purpose.
I heard your voice,
I accepted your plea,

Your offering greatly pleases Me.
You are Mine!
I AM yours
Pure Joy!

Come and dance with Me,
For the joy I see in your face
Is a reflection of My joy in you

Freely given
Humbly offered
Giving joy

Pure Joy!

Jesus

The Rewarder

I AM a rewarder of those who seek Me.
I will be found in abundance by the honest.
I reveal the treasure of My wisdom
To those without guile.
Through them, My nature is revealed.

Whosoever will may know Me if they seek.
Those with no agenda, too receive a peek.
To those who tarry, waiting, I will speak
Truth, eternal truth, they will seek.

Be careful what you ask for,
Be honest when you call.
Remember I AM with you,
Redeemed you from The Fall.

When questioned, answer clearly.
Your eyes will tell it all:
The Truth.
Eternal . . . Truth.

I am the Rewarder.
Could anything be clearer
Than truth revealed by God,
Depending on the hearer.
Relationship of laud.

How can you know the Shearer
Unless as sheep you've trod?
Know thy Rewarder.
Then, know the Truth: I AM God.

Seek Me.
    I AM the Rewarder.

Jesus

Draw Nigh

There is a way to come to God.
The cost is faith and time.
Your faith then it draws Me close to you
I whisper, "You are Mine."

The cost to you who make this choice
Is minutes fully spent
To turn away from life's demands,
To listen, pray, repent.

And when you have My Word before you,
Hear Me deep inside,
You pull from Me as without effort
Connection that abides.

I meet you early, hear your heart,
I know of life's demands,
Encourage you, give brand new start,
Break off the worry bands.

While you take time to come and meet,
It's like your life's on hold,
For nothing can approach you here,
You're safe within the fold.

And any time throughout the day
When trouble rises tall,
Look up to Me, remembering
That I AM Lord of All.

My Peace I give when yours depletes,
Reminds I'm still with you,
And you remember days gone by
When I was with you too.

This simple act of drawing nigh
In early light of day,
Like wearing armor to the war
I go before this way.

My Peace now settles, brings you back
From yawning pit of worry.
Trust rises up, brings forth the calm,
Releases need to hurry.

And I will meet you each new day
It's like we meet on high.
You will settle, meditate,
As you reach out, draw nigh.

And I draw nigh to you.

Jesus

Walking Redeemed

Blessed and beloved
Holy by My blood
Cool and sweet the breezes
Day before the flood

In this life are heartache,
Stumbles, wrong, and woe
But I'm walking with you
Everywhere you go

Trouble often multiplies
Coming fast and hard
Remedies and answers
Just aren't in the cards

Hope is what I give you
Comfort for the way
Blessed Hope in Jesus
Like a sunshine ray

You walk through the trial
Holding to My hand
I AM surely leading
To the Promised Land

Life is overwhelming
Difficult at best
Yet there are oases
Where I give you rest

Laughter, peace and joy come
Children grace your lap
Food and drink are plenty
You may e'en grow fat

Soon may come promotion
Valued worker you
All is well, it's easy
From your point of view

Life is at its best here
Everything your way
Then the years get harder
Notice that I stay

Within, without, with nothing
Life comes difficult
Body may betray you
End in wrong result

Beloved I AM with you
When you are alone
Comfort, peace I give you
Then I take you home.

Jesus

Father

Living in God's Love

As far as the heavens
And beyond into space,
As far as great galaxies
Unseen by your eyes,

Surrounding you always
Before and behind,
I AM your Savior
And God only wise.

All through your life
I have been by your side:
Struggles and anguish,
And joy beyond measure,

Triumph, disaster,
Ire fit to be tied,
Great loss and sorrow,
Excitement, My treasure.

No one else knows
Your small thoughts as I do.
No one else cares anyway.

Only your heavenly
Father knows why,
What it means,
"I'm the Truth and the Way."

Softer and quieter,
With bated breath,
You just can't wait
To spend time with me.

You learn of My treasures
Of wisdom in scripture,
Aware Spirit's leading
And you want to see.

It is enough that you
Know for yourself,
Yet you feel pressed
To share Me with any.

I AM your Secret,
Seen with closed eyes:
Father and Lord,
Spirit to many.

Rejoice in salvation,
Know that I AM.
Nothing will keep us apart.

Capture My Love
In mere words here on paper.
Waiting, expecting, it starts.

The day stands before you:
Treasure to discover,
Mishaps and slipups included.

Know I AM with you
Whatever may come
All quiet time has preluded.

Step out and live!

Father

Every Life

Child, you are a wonder.
Quick to forgive others,
Forgiving yourself is hard for you.
I AM here for that.
You can trust Me in all things — Always.

Nothing is too difficult when you are in Christ.
You can do all things through Me.
In fact, there is nothing you can do without Me,
For by Me all things consist and have their being.

You may ask Me anything.
Ask Me *for* anything in My Name
And you will have what you ask
When you ask in faith . . and wait.

Is that too hard for you to take in?
To comprehend?
To wrap your mind around?

Nothing can separate you from My Love.
That is because I AM in every cell, every Atom,
And there is no way to separate us
And you still exist.

Nothing exists without Me.
All things are made of matter
And matter is energy.
I AM energy, light, life.

And yet . . .
Until a person believes that I AM
And connects to Me by faith,
They remain in darkness.

Faith is like a light switch.
It brings the latent energy in you to life
When faith is activated.

Even your countenance is changed
Your whole being is full of light . . .
Me in you, making you
Alive to the Truth.

Every lamp has a switch.
Every soul has been given
A measure of faith.
Every life has a purpose:

Some for destruction, some for My glory,
Yet whosoever will may come.
It is a choice.

Father

My Treasure

Your love is My measure,
My absolute treasure.
I get plenty of fear and lots of requests
But your love is My absolute treasure.

I yearn over you, loving you without rest,
Receiving your awe and your fear.
Your worship and praise is so very precious.
I catch them and save every tear.

My love for all flesh is strong and it's true
And I reach out to you every way.
Some hear and respond,
Others' fear keeps them bound,
Even those who deny me have grace.

I AM God and I stand without need in all things.
I love every one but owe no one My hand
For My Son reigns forever King of kings.

All I want, I create. All I see already Mine.
Every treasure of man I have made.
There is nothing required to complete
Yet to you, invitation is laid.

Mankind may receive invitation.
People I bid to My throne.
Man, woman, child are completed by Me
Understand when in heaven are known.

Enough to complete all of creation
To raise up, throw down, tribes and nations,
And though I AM sovereign,
A prayer stays my hand.

My praise on the lips
Of those in every land
Brings My presence
And power to the moment.

And your life is changed
When you too declare
Jesus is Lord, not opponent.

Though some will turn back,
Many others pray through
All temptation and trial and pain.

And their joy is much stronger,
Their love is more sure
Just because they
Have been born again.

Father

Those

Beloved, those who come to Me
Have long been loved by Me.
I AM Love.

In spite of your choices,
I hold you to life
Till your number of days is completed.
All have problems. That is life.

Those who blame cannot see
What I have guided them around,
Brought them through,
Lifted them above, shielded them from.

Those who blame,
Who see themselves as victims,
Give their power away,
Justify their lies of pain,
Rail at Me.

They see no benefit in knowing Me.
They have no reference
That would indicate I AM good.
They do not believe.

When you tell them of
The good I have done in your life,
Their filter of experience
Provides no recognition or connection.

And they may say,
"Good for you," or "yeah, *right*."
They think God has chosen some
And ignored the rest, including them.

They cannot hear the Good News.
Though they have heard of Jesus,
They do not know the Truth
And only Truth can set them free.

Pray for them.

Those who are thankful
Own their problems,
Take responsibility for their actions,
Help others, and are generous.

The bad things in their lives are looked at
As happening for a reason.
They look for good to follow.

They are thankful for what they have
And for what they receive.
These are they who hear the Good News
Of Jesus Christ

And believe it to be Truth.
Rejoice with them.

I AM. I do not conform
To anyone's idea of God.
I simply AM. Let those who will, come.
I will lead them into Truth.

I will cause My Light to shine into them
And they will *know* Me experientially.
Then they will know the Truth,
And the Truth will set them free.

Be thankful with them.

You are such a one.
Continue to be thankful,
For that is great praise.

Father

Conviction

There are certain things
I convict you of.
I point them out
Because of Love.

They trip you up,
Though seem benign
Innocuous looking,
But they can bind.

I want you free
To come and sit,
Each thought and word
A wholesome bit.

The things you know
That trip you up
Can constitute
A bitter cup.

The reason
I tell you no
Will make your walk
An easier go.

I see ahead.
I know your heart.
I'd spare you pain
Right from the start.

But habits set
That friends expect
Can drag you back.
Sin is a net.

Then you will hear
The enemy's way:
"Dear friend,
Did God *Really* say?"

I want to spare
You compromise
And though you're perfect
In My eyes,

The things you said
And did before
May now lay crouching
At your door

To trap you.

If they do,
Just shake them off.
Repent despite
Old friends who scoff.

Return to Me
And we'll walk on.
Eventually,
Regret is gone.

But there's a scar
From enemy's skirmish.
Just wear it proudly
As it grows firmish.

For it proclaims
In realms unseen
You're born again,
Say what you mean.

You're Mine.

Father

Struggle

Why is it necessary to struggle?
Because of sin.
Even the blessings of God require work
And care
And assembling
And prayer.
Those who refuse the struggle,
Who won't toil,
Are those who will not reap with joy.

They find life too hard,
Don't want to grow up,
Have no depth,
Wait on others to deploy.
They will never find satisfaction.
Then, when those of them who believe
Come to judgment,
Their talents will not have multiplied.

Investing your gifts in doing for Me,
You will meet resistance
And failure
And hard work for little gain.

When you meet with poor outcome,
You are doing just fine.
Though life is a struggle,
The alternative is not better.
Keep going.

I have called you to
A deep understanding of Me.
That requires hard work:
Inconvenience
Courage
Embarrassment
Time in My Word
Study
Seeking My Face
Worship
Prayer
Patience
False starts
Mistakes
And beginning again
Time after time after time.

Keep coming.
The struggle is worth it.
Oh, so worth it!

Father

Going

Many trials are in the mind
Wrong turns there bring fear
Answers delayed deplete the hope
Obfuscate what should be clear

Time in waiting here on the Lord
No answer comes, denied.
Faith sustains, brings comfort, seals
Trust God, not doubts implied

No answer given, some turn away
But there is no Plan B
You wait and trust, and trust and wait
Continue to worship Me

I'm drawing you to deeper wells
Where you must walk out faith
I'm leading you up steeper paths
Where you will need more grace

This is the place you might be wrong,
Must follow anyway
This is the time when you will choose
Belief o'er what men say

Here the answers won't come easy
May not come at all
Here you choose who you'll believe
Here you stand or fall

Will you follow? Will you serve Me?
Will you eat my flesh?
Will you drink My blood, remember
When your faith was fresh?

This is long road through the desert
Here the path runs out
This is where the thirst o'ertakes you
This is what life's all about

Living loved, you take for granted
Tomorrow will be like today
You've got to know that takes no faith
Required trials lead other way

Don't sit and wait for this to pass
Get up and follow Me
Deep or shallow faith determined
By believing what you can't see.

Hard or easy? Right or wrong?
Come on, get up. We're going.

Father

Hiding

There are things that are hidden
That I'll bring to light
The lost will be found
And be seen in plain sight

There's nothing worth losing
That can't be replaced
Until we are talking
Of souls who need grace.

So many who wonder
Why others can't see
God in the clouds
And the times yet to be

Those who are hiding
Will soon realize
The earth is the Lord's
In His hand are the skies

And nothing is hidden
That won't be explained
For all who will come
Are saved with no blame.

What's hiding will open
Revealing through grace
How souls who are waiting
Will see Jesus' face

And will come out of hiding.

Father

Take Time to Be Holy

Take time to be holy
Look to Me in your day
Sit in your chair and
Know I am there
I AM the Truth and the Way

Take time now to listen
Focus, My words in your mind
When you focus on Me
Heav'n's Holy Three
I AM the One God you'll find

Take time to be still now
Wait silent and hear
Quietly breathe
Here on your knees
Open to Holy drawn near

Take time to be waiting
Come expecting to stay
Your time I'll anoint
I don't disappoint
New strength
You receive for the day

You've strength for the climb
Quite enough for this time
Take time to be holy and see

My Grace is sufficient
I know every care
Whatever you bear,
Bring to Me

Answers arrive
Your spirit revives
Because you've spent time
Here with Me.

Just remember . . .
Take time to be holy.

Father

Spend Time with My Son

Great peace then goes with you
All the day long.
Relaxed, fresh, you smile at
Whatever goes wrong.

My Presence stays with you
Wherever you go
And others may notice
You just warmly glow.

The hard knocks of life
Will not set you adrift
In worry, then grasping
To quick mend a rift.

You'll see this life's troubles
As small and will wait
As short prayer refocus
Leads you calm in faith.

It's harder to hear
My soft voice in your mind.
When morning news comes,
You leave Me behind.

So, seek in the early
While Savior awaits
To give you My Peace
To face life-storming gates.

You've nothing to lose
And all heaven to gain.
As you wait in My Presence
I take all your pain.

And here in the dark
I will meet you who come
In faith stepping forward
To meet with God's Son.

Fresh blessings enfold you
And Grace takes your hand.
Leading and guiding
I'll cause you to stand.

Knowing you are Mine
Remembering I AM yours

Strong . . in faith
Sure . . . of your salvation
True . . . because you want more
Ready . . because you are
Hidden in Christ . . . Forever.

Believing

Just Love Me

Beloved, welcome into My open arms.
You build spiritual strength
When you present yourself open to Me.
You bring Me joy with your thoughts of Me.

Your spoken words to Me are often
A continuation of what you are thinking
A conversation . . .
Easily misinterpreted by others.

So what?
You are in fairly constant
Communication with Me
And that trumps everything.

Just love Me, child.
Keep on loving Me,
For I AM with you no matter what.
I PROMISE.

Jesus

This Life

All are important in shaping each other
When I AM at work in the lives of mankind.
And I'm ever working, My Spirit hovers.
As each, every trial brings wisdom to find.

Wisdom or knowledge? There is no difference.
One is applied, the other accrues.
Every experience actually matters.
No little piece is left out, for I choose.

What you go through
Brings strength you don't notice
Until problem crops up again.
Then you have answer, know how to proceed
With confident caution, to expected end.

But when you don't know
What to do from experience,
Then you must wait, look to Me.
And waiting's not easy,
You want to take action
With what comes to hand that you see.

Your hand is your answer,
You've fixed things before,
Ready, apply what you've learned.

And I often watch as you do it your own way
Instead of waiting on Me for the turn.

That's why do-overs are covered by Grace.
You rush while I steadily lead.
And when you come to the answer deferred,
Know all things come at their own speed.

Things that are rushed spiral out of control,
Seem to take on a life of their own.
Meanwhile, I'm working in background unseen
Would I give you no fish but a stone?

Of course not.

Wisdom or knowledge?
Well, just wait and see.
Let me lead you directly to end.
If you are quite willing to wait on my speed,
You'll see blessings come round the bend.

It's rather like dancing, this life I have given,
Much smoother when you let Me lead.
Each, every newborn must learn of these rules.
Knowledge turns wisdom indeed.

Take My hand.
Let us walk together,
For *there* is wisdom.

Father

Blessings Abound

Not every blessing is obvious
But looking back, becomes plain.
Dodged a bullet many times
Whether realized or not.

I've led you into trial
When needed for your growth.
Sometimes, when it was behind
You, you thanked Me.

Often, you've looked up and smiled.
Other times brought you
To your knees in tears.
And through it all, you trusted Me.

Forgetting.
But daily blessings still Abound
As I lead, guide, and direct.

Walk with Me now into old age
And find the treasures awaiting.

My words are still "Follow Me."

So, Shine

Daughter One, you are Mine
Always Mine, Ever Mine

Nothing can separate you from My Love.
Hearts grow cold when life comes between.
It takes dedication, determination
To be faithful to One unseen.

Every day it's a decision
What do first, what not forget.
When you come to me on waking
I know Mine and I direct.

Commanding blessing on any who love Me
One who is faithful to seek Me out
One who waits to do My bidding
Praying soft or singing, shout

It is so precious My Love astounds you
For you wait and then I fill
With My Presence all around you
I go with you, on others spill.

Shine for Me, carry My Presence
To the ones you will meet today.
For you glow from My light within you
Others notice along the way.

As you ponder truths imparted,
Keep a smile wherever you go.
Others meet you, those who know Me
Recognize My Presence flows

Through you.
    From Me.
        So, Shine!

Father

Open Your Heart

I have been pouring My love out on you.
But you haven't been receiving it.
Open your heart – plese let Me come in.
Behold I stand at the door and knock.

Now, as you open the door,
You keep Me a guest in the foyer.
Invite Me into your life, your being.
Your fear of inadequacy keeps us apart.

I *know* your heart.

Invite Me into the dining room
That we might sup together.
Invite Me into the kitchen
That we might work together.

Invite Me into the bathroom
That we might know each other.
Invite Me into the bedroom
That our secrets may be shared.

You hide your secrets and let none know.
But I know already.
Until you let Me share your secrets,
I cannot let you share Mine.

Only then can we fellowship.
Only then can you worship Me
In Spirit and Truth.
For you do not yet have the truth.
Just stop. Open your heart. Let Me in.

Come to Me and rest.
I am easy to approach
And you are sure of your welcome,
Sure of Me,
Knowing I will receive all who
Call on My Name.
So, what is worrying you now?

You can't know the future!
Preparing for meetings and appointments
Is one thing, but controlling what will take
place next is a myth, a dream, a what-if.

Quit it! All your planning and worry
Leaves Me out of the equation.
And, of course, I AM talking to the wind.

The thing to remember is
I AM with you.
Let that be enough.

Love Does Not

It does not. No. It doesn't.
Love does not run away; it hangs in there.
Love is looking for the good that will follow.
Love believes in happy endings, so it waits,
Believing in good.

Love does not envy. It is generous
And appreciates another's blessings,
Rejoicing for that one's joy.
Love does not play games.

Jealousy doesn't live here, for there is no
Room within love to be jealous.
Love would have to cease, to stop,
To allow jealousy any room at all.
No, Love doesn't thrive
Where there is jealousy.

Love does not boast. It doesn't.
It has no need to draw attention to itself,
For it is complete, having more than enough
So it can generously give love away.

Love cannot be puffed up,
For it does not even need to be noticed.
Love is self-provisioning. It is enough.
It does not need. It gives.

Love does not behave rudely
Because it never insists on its rights.
It *is* right.

Love does not seek its own.
It *is* its own, having all it needs,
Every requirement satisfied,
Always ready to focus on others.

Love does not become provoked.
Love does not entertain negative thoughts.
It remains focused on loving
In positive, healthy, live-giving ways.

And negativity withers.

Love does not think on nor dwell on evil.
There is simply no interest.
Darkness and light cannot dwell together.

Love does not get pleasure
From another's misfortune.
To do that, Love would
Have to be needy itself.
And it isn't.

Love bears all things,
Not with a "this too shall pass" attitude,
But believing all things work together
For good to them that love.

Love always hopes.
Always.
It never weakens.

Love does not fail. It is perfect.
It is, in fact, the only thing in this world
That *is* perfect.

God is Love.

I Corinthians 13:4-7
Romans 8:28
John 4:8

Wait on Me

You have been busy
Doing many things
But have accomplished little.
You need to wait on Me.

I will accomplish everything you seek
But it will be in My time
In My way
And you will stand still and watch
And will see the salvation of the Lord.

You strive for and try hard
And accomplish little
I am able to lay it in your lap.

During this time of testing
Lean on Me
Let Me be your strength.

Trust Me just a little longer
Just a little farther
Just a little deeper
Just a little more.

Let Me fill up
That which is lacking
Let Me be your focus
Make Me your purpose

And see what I can do
Through you, for you
With you, by you
Stop now all the worry
Be anxious for nothing

Ask for what you need
And it will be supplied

Sleep more, rest in Me
Sing more, sing My praise
Not because I need it
But because of
What it does inside you

Let Me change you
From the inside
And continue the work
I have begun in you.
Set aside time to pray

Time to worship
Time in the Word
And time for reflection.

Now, while you have
Time on your hands
Give Me your time
And see what I will do

Let me show you off
I want others to see
The rewards available
To one who will allow Me
To fill them with My Spirit

As you wait on Me
Let Me do
What I want to do

Let Me . . .
Let Me . . .
Let Me . . .

While you wait.

Father

Whenever

Whenever you need Me, I'm already there,
Leading and guiding, addressing each care.
When words fly faster than you even think,
Reaction much stronger, you fight without blink.

There in the midst of the cutting, harsh words,
Spirit reminds you of what you have heard:
Put on, wear mercy as chosen and loved,
Patience and gentleness yours from above.

Dig out long-suffering, choose to forgive,
Endure wrong tirelessly, Christ in you lives.
Bind up the broken heart, give it to Him,
Allow His words in you the breakout to end.

You may not have the guts to stop and say
I need time out to let God have His way.
But when it is over, He's with you inside.
Say, Friend, I'm sorry – please tell your side.

Notice the rhythm and cadence of words
Slows for reflection on motives heart stirred.
You give respect to this one you face
Anger dies quiet as you apply grace.

This opportunity sets this one free
So listen long, hear him turn to Me.
Come now into the sun – hear loud and clear.
Spirit gives grace so this one can hear.

Then let your answer affirm him in love,
This one who's wanted by Holy above.
Grace I have showered on just and unjust.
Man is the best thing I made from the Earth dust.

Trust Me . . .
    Whenever you need Me,
        I AM with you.

Father

Tithing is Faith

Nothing can keep you from Me, I AM Love.
Nothing can separate spirit from Spirit.
Once you surrender and ask Me to come,
I speak of Love. In your heart; you can hear it.

As you live daily, you see Me in all:
Everywhere, everything
Seen through new eyes.
You come to understand nothing is chance.
Blessings and trials come fast, any size.

Faith, I have given, small mustard seed new,
Unfolds and takes root in your heart.
"Try Me," I said in My Word, and you do,
And find money's the place where we start.

Ten cents is Mine, you don't want to rob God.
It's simple at first 'cause the dollars are few.
Then as faith grows, you rejoice in abundance
And tithing gets harder 'cause those dollars
Grew!

So now tests of faith are bigger, cost more,
But faith has grown stronger inside.
Faith has brought answers
To prayers you have prayed:
Health, spouse, kids, job strong faith tried.

Those lost through death grieved your soul
But you found comfort from Me
Brought you through.
Nothing can separate you from My Love.
You learned that each day's a new gift for you.

You see My hand clearly is leading your life.
You trust Me in everything though I'm unseen.
You've learned bad things happen
And good things do too
And know I AM good, I'm not mean.

A pattern of giving, established and set,
You tithe and you offer and give.
Now I invite and I lead you to grow,
Launch into the deep, by faith live.

I still hold your hand and I sure won't let go
Every time your feet slipped,
It 'twas My hand that caught 'em.
You prove every payday
Who's Lord of your life
'Cause tithing is faith … signed at the bottom.

Father

Unseen Power

About Angels

Precious, I see you.
I personally watch over you.
My angels are charged
With watching over you.
They personally answer to Me
For your safety.

Can you imagine them knowing
All about you,
Yet never having an opinion
About each and every thought
You have and action you take?

Imagine, too, the everlasting
Love of God they are
Coming constantly to you,
Hovering over you,
Walking with you,
Lifting you from regret,
Going before and behind you,
And gently watching over you
Every day you live.

They are beings of light who serve Me
By serving you every day.
They are one of the many ways
I express My Love to You.

I AM in you thoroughly,
Each cell and corpuscle created by Me
To keep you alive,
Each breath of your body
Provided through Me.

These angels are expressions of I AM.
They are powerful, invisible
Expressions of My Love for you
Sent with your spirit at conception,
Charged with Me, Energy unseen.

Ah, this explanation is too wonderful
For you to comprehend. That's OK.
When you come to me in heaven,
You will know what you know don't yet.

What you do not now understand
Will all be known.
All will be revealed.

"Now we know in part"
When I bring you to Me,
Everything will make perfect sense.
I promise.

For now, just remember that I love you
And will never leave you nor forsake you.
I won't change My mind.

And no circumstances will alter
The love and peace you walk in.
You are My vessel,
Chosen for My work in you,
In the earth.

How about this? *"Just roll with it."*

You don't have to understand to believe.
Have a good day

Author

Karen J Chisholm

Lives in a suburb of Houston, Texas.

She occasionally speaks about her experiences listening to Father in the early morning. It is from these mornings Karen writes the words she "hears" in conversations with God through Holy Spirit.

Since God is unseen, it is easier to write word by word God's message through Holy Spirit, thereby not interrupting the flow of encouragement being released.

These words are usually passed down in the form of poetry using a simple pencil on everyday paper, thus making the eternal known to those who will believe.

Sparkling Waters is the sixth book now in hands around the world per Father's direction.